Tecumseh

CHERRY LAKE PRESS

Published in the United States of America by Cherry Lake Publishing Group
Ann Arbor, Michigan
www.cherrylakepublishing.com

Reading Adviser: Beth Walker Gambro, MS, Ed., Reading Consultant, Yorkville, IL
Book Designer: Jennifer Wahi
Illustrator: Jeff Bane

Photo Credits: page 5: © Kenneth Keifer/Shutterstock; page 7: © Morphart Creation/Shutterstock; pages 9, 17, 23: © Everett Collection/Shutterstock; pages 11, 22: Indiana Department of Natural Resources; page 13: © National Portrait Gallery, Smithsonian Institution; page 15: Library of Congress, Prints and Photographs Division; page 19: © Joyce Nelson/Shutterstock; page 21: © Les Winkeler

Cherry Lake Press is an imprint of Cherry Lake Publishing Group.

Library of Congress Cataloging-in-Publication Data

Names: Thiele, June, author. | Bane, Jeff, 1957- illustrator.
Title: Tecumseh / written by: June Thiele ; illustrated by: Jeff Bane.
Description: Ann Arbor, Michigan : Cherry Lake Publishing, [2023] | Series: My itty-bitty bio | Includes index. | Audience: Grades K-1 | Summary: "This biography for early readers examines the life of Shawnee chief and warrior Tecumseh in a simple, age-appropriate way that helps young readers develop word recognition and reading skills. Includes table of contents, author biography, timeline, glossary, index, and other informative backmatter. The My Itty-Bitty Bio series celebrates diversity, covering women and men from a range of backgrounds and professions including immigrants and individuals with disabilities"-- Provided by publisher.
Identifiers: LCCN 2022042723 | ISBN 9781668919187 (hardcover) | ISBN 9781668920206 (paperback) | ISBN 9781668921531 (ebook) | ISBN 9781668922866 (pdf)
Subjects: LCSH: Tecumseh, Shawnee Chief, 1768-1813--Juvenile literature. | Shawnee Indians--Kings and rulers--Biography--Juvenile literature. | Indians of North America--Wars--1812-1815--Juvenile literature.
Classification: LCC E99. S35 T349 2023 | DDC 977.004/973170092 [B]--dc23/eng/20220912
LC record available at https://lccn.loc.gov/2022042723

Printed in the United States of America
Corporate Graphics

About the author: June Thiele writes and acts in Chicago where they live with their wife and child. June is Dena'ina Athabascan and Yup'ik, Indigenous cultures of Alaska. They try to get back home to Alaska as much as possible.

About the illustrator: Jeff Bane and his two business partners own a studio along the American River in Folsom, California, home of the 1849 Gold Rush. When Jeff's not sketching or illustrating for clients, he's either swimming or kayaking in the river to relax.

I was born in 1768 in Ohio. I am **Native American**. I am **Shawnee**.

My father died when I was young. My older sister raised me and my **siblings**.

I saw **colonizers** steal our land. I wanted to fight back. I was brave. I became a chief of my people.

What do you stand up for?

My brother and I created a town.
It was called Prophetstown.
We wanted to **protect** our way
of life.

I wanted to **unite** tribes. I knew we would be stronger together.
I traveled to different states.
I met with many leaders.
We were building a united community.

While I was away, colonizers attacked Prophetstown. They destroyed it.

GENERAL HARRISON
THE WASHINGTON OF THE WEST.

The colonizers went to war with Great Britain. My people teamed up with Great Britain. We wanted to defeat the **settlers**.

Many tribes joined us. We worked together. We wanted our land back from the settlers. We won many battles.

NATIVE ALLIES

In addition to the Six Nations named on the limestone walls, the members of these Native Nations also took part in the War of 1812:

ALLIES AUTOCHTONES

En plus des Six Nations nommées sur les murs de calcaire, les membres de ces nations autochtones ont également participé à la guerre de 1812:

Abenaki of Three Rivers and St. Francis
Algonquin
Anishnaabeg
Akwesasne Mohawk
Cherokee
Dakotah (Sioux)
Delaware
Fox
Huron of Lorette
Kahnawake Mohawk
Kanesatake Mohawk
Kickapoo
Menominee
Mesquakie

Métis
Miami
Mississauga
Mohican
Moravian
Muncey
Nanticoke
Odawa
Ojibwe
Potowatomi
Sauk
Shawnee
Tyendinaga Mohawk
Winnebago (Ho Chunk)
Wyandot

What groups are you part of?

19

I died in 1813 during a battle. But my legacy continues. I inspire people to work together.

What would you like to ask me?

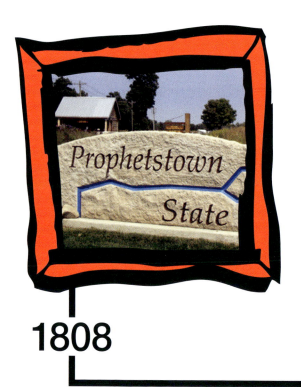

1808

1760

Born
1768

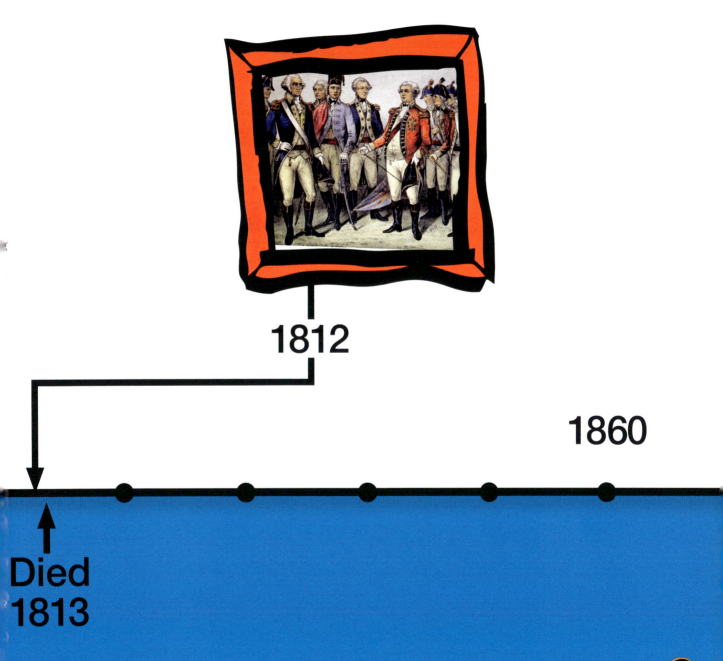

1812

1860

Died
1813

glossary

colonizers (KAH-luh-ny-zuhrs) people who take control of another people or country

Native American (NAY-tiv uh-MEHR-uh-kuhn) one of the people who originally lived on the land that became the United States, or a relative of these people

settlers (SET-luhrz) people who move with a group of others to live in a new country or area

Shawnee (shah-NEE) member of a North American people living formerly in the eastern United States and now mainly in Oklahoma

siblings (SIH-blings) brothers and sisters

unite (yoo-NYT) to come or bring together for a common purpose or action

index